YOUNG KING

TAKE YOUR STAND

Dexter A. Powell, Jr.

Cover Design: ICHD Designs

ISBN: 978-1-952926-03-7

Printed in the United States of America

Manifold Grace Publishing House, LLC
Southfield, Michigan 48033
www.manifoldgracepublishinghouse.com

MANIFOLD GRACE
Publishing House LLC

DEDICATION

This book is dedicated to my daughter, Kayla. My one decision, at twelve years old, ultimately ended up affecting your life and for that I apologize. I will spend my future showing you what redemption looks like and how, if you make your next decision your best decision, you can change your life forever.

To the memory of my grandmothers,

Maggie Lucendia Powell
(12/18/1938 - 9/9/2011)
and
Yolanda Garibaldi Jefferson
(11/25/1937 – 11/17/2017)

I hope my work in the world makes you both proud.

I love you!

ACKNOWLEDGMENTS

To say this has been quite the journey would be the understatement of a lifetime. Young King was birthed out of years of pain and misery. Since childhood I've suffered because of my own bad decisions. My life felt purposeless because I was hopeless, sick, addicted, broken, lost, and clinically depressed. That was a lie. I am a King and I have come to take my stand.

Thank you to my rock, Breona. You have loved me through all my mess and eventually helped me cultivate my message to the world.

I am so grateful for the angel who birthed me some thirty-eight years ago. Mom, this book would not exist if it hadn't been for you making grueling decisions for my ultimate good.

Kayla, prepare to soar higher than ever before as you take your stand in life and find all that lives within you.

Thank you to those who have supported my journey from behind the scenes.

To my publisher, Darlene, who has implored me to write, write, write for over a decade. Well, I finally have one on the shelf!

To my editor, Tenita "Bestseller" Johnson, for editing the contents of my heart.

This is just the beginning, enjoy the read.

TABLE OF CONTENTS

INTRO:
OUR JOURNEY
BEGINS

Hello, young kings. As you read these pages, my prayer is that you become more aware of who you are and your place in this world. But beware: someone else is already thinking of how they can tear you down. That stops today because you are about to become equipped for a greater purpose. Young king, arise and take your stand!

I don't know where you are on your life's journey. But I am fairly certain that since waking up this morning, someone or something has gotten under your skin. It's all good. We all lose our cool at times. However, what happens when you lose your cool? What choices do you make in the heat of the moment? These are just a couple of questions to ask yourself as our young king journey begins.

It's vital that you know you are valued, you are loved, and you are very much needed. Young king, you have so much to give our world. As you begin to take your stand, you will become the earth's greatest asset toward a better, more unified future. The path to nowhere is easy to find. Our world offers so many readily available options to ease our pain and distract us from that which we may be feeling from day to day. We may find ourselves using these easy options to fill empty spaces in our soul. But ultimately, this only results in roadblocks, dead-end seasons of frustration, and great internal pain. This causes the collapse of your royal kingship. That's why I'm here: to guide you along this new quest of becoming an *authentic young king*.

I applaud you for reading this book and taking the opportunity to stand up for yourself and your life. You come from a royal bloodline. You were born to dominate in this world. You, my friend, are a young king. You are a game changer. You are a life elevator. We need you to arise and take your stand *now*!

CHAPTER 1

WHEN I'M HUNGRY, I STEAL

At the age of twelve, in San Bernardino, California, I stood in the front yard of my house screaming at the top of my lungs, "Mom, please make them take these handcuffs off me!" But, at that point, it was too late.

The previous year, my parents had gone through a bad divorce. My mom and me, along with my younger brother, Mars, moved into a tiny house owned by my grandfather.

I was in the sixth grade at Warm Springs Elementary School and I was now the "man of the house." Life was rather good, as far as I was concerned. I took great pride in the fact that my mom and brother had to depend on me to take care of them. Boy, was I young and immature.

Sixth grade was weird because my body was changing. I was already struggling with an out-of-control food addiction. I kept rapidly outgrowing the clothes my mother bought for me. Food was my life. I ate every chance I got, even when I wasn't hungry. I stole food from everywhere, including my home, from my peers, and grocery markets. No location was safe if I was around and there was food in the room.

I had a lot of pain in my young age. I ate just so I could comfort my aching soul. Daily I stole and ate until I was sick and unable to move. Yet, I still wanted more. Every chew gave me an intense rush that I couldn't explain.

I was bullied because of my size. I was, by far, the biggest kid in my class. I looked much older than my classmates. So, to me, I always felt like the verbal abuse I received was justified, although I now know that was a falsehood. The more my tormenters and peers teased me, the more food I stole and consumed. This self-destructive pattern set me up for a life of struggle and hopelessness, which I could have never imagined.

One afternoon, Mars and I were walking home from school when I decided that I needed to eat something, anything, and quick because I'd had a stressful day. Unfortunately, we didn't have any money. But that didn't stop our pursuit. We walked into the corner store, Jolly Boys. I planned to steal some Little Debbie snacks so I could settle my ravaging desire to eat. Mars played the lookout as I stole three boxes of snack cakes for our afternoon snack. This was a common practice that I used in some form or fashion every day somewhere. I had become a kleptomaniac of food.

Believing I had gotten away scot-free gave me hope that I could continue these practices for life. The adrenaline rush I received from stealing snacks was absolutely amazing. Keep in mind that this was before the advent of social media. So, sneaking around and stealing food was one of the main ways I kept myself entertained as a young, misguided king.

My daily pursuits of thievery birthed an addiction, not only to eating, but to stealing, as well. More than anything, not getting caught always gave me a great feeling, which I became addicted to. It almost rivaled chewing and the cortisol that flowed from my brain when I ate. I would drift off into a state of utter bliss with each bite of my strawberry shortcake rolls and oatmeal pies. I repeated this process, smashing snacks without regard for my ever-growing frame. Stealing opened a window that year. It created a habit that was meant to destroy my young kingship. I was led down the wrong path quickly because of my choices. I walked down roads I did not want to travel, but I had no control over myself. However, my inability to control myself, and my thieving ways and decisions, soon backfired.

KING'S SPOTLIGHT

I am a young king.

I am unstoppable.

I rise in the face of adversity.

I am loved.

I am valued.

I am needed.

I won't be stopped.

I can't be stopped.

I am a young king.

CHAPTER 2
MEETING MR. BELL

One day when Mars and I had returned home from school, my mom introduced us to her "friend," Mr. Bell. He was in his late twenties and was fresh out of the Air Force. He was a well-dressed black man and he smelled of expensive cologne. I was not impressed with his appearance. His infatuation with my mother was a huge red flag for me. You must remember that I had just been recently self-appointed as the man of our house. I vowed to do everything in my power to run him off into the wind, screaming with his tail between his legs. However, he was stronger than I originally anticipated, and his strength superseded my attempts at rebellion.

When the initial introduction happened, I felt like my mother had slapped me right in the face. I thought, *How dare she bring this man into our lives?* I had our house under control. There was no need for any additional outside testosterone in our small home. We only had enough room for the three of us. Now, we were forced to make room for another. My mind switched to a mode of pure evil thoughts and intentions because of his invasion into our lives.

In no time, Mr. Bell moved a few things in that he could fit in our small home. He was a very educated, staunch disciplinarian. Apparently, that was also the way he was raised—under an iron fist and military restrictions. This type of adjustment did not sit well in my soul. I tried to sabotage their relationship at every turn because I wanted my domain back. I wanted Mr. Bell to be gone and quickly. One day, my mother even chased me down the street, trying to whoop me for attempting to run off Mr. Bell by my many mischievous antics. I was trying to reach the crevices of his anger, causing him to reach a point of explosion in which he would leave my mother for good. However, it never happened.

School became increasingly more difficult by the day. I had a tough time concentrating long enough to learn effectively. I was too busy messing around talking to my nearest peers, often telling jokes, and trying to deflect attention away from my weight. I was labeled fat, ugly, and stupid by my peers. For the most part, I believed every word that others spoke over my life. I endured so many mean and obscene fat jokes each day at school. The bullying I faced, coupled with my choice to rebel against the system and my mother, derailed my life at the tender age of twelve.

One sunny afternoon, my mother informed us that she and Mr. Bell were getting married. The sky immediately darkened over my world. Everything changed in that moment. I had many thoughts up until that point about whether my mother absolutely loved me. When she delivered the news of their impending nuptials, I received a direct revelation in my spirit that this woman must really hate me if she would choose to marry him over Mars and me. In my inexperience, I had made up my mind that I was going to do my own thing. Neither him, nor my mother, was going to run or ruin my life from that point on.

Mr. Bell began working as a biology teacher at the local high school. He was also the advisor of the Black Student Union (BSU). One weekend, the BSU sponsored a student car wash. They had a great turnout and made a lot of money. Mr. Bell brought the earnings home for safe keeping until school resumed. He placed the money in their bedroom closet in a coffee tin, where he thought it would remain safe until Monday. But that wasn't the case.

I watched him like a hawk from the moment I saw him with the money. Once Mr. Bell secured the funds, and felt confident with his choice hiding location, I helped myself to sixty dollars. Honestly, I couldn't tell you why I stole it. But I did. Then, I returned to the hiding spot several more times. By the end of the night, the coffee tin that once held the money was empty. The contents were safely hidden under my bed. I'd made big plans for that money the following Monday at school. I'd made great big plans, mainly based around purchasing food.

KING'S SPOTLIGHT

Today, I will choose to make my next decision my best decision. I am fully aware that someone in this world does not want me to succeed. Thankfully, their wants don't dictate my outcome in life. Despite them, I will be successful at everything I put my full effort toward.

CHAPTER 3
BIG MAN ON CAMPUS

On Monday morning, I woke up full of confidence because I knew that I was going to be the big man on campus. I had a pocket full of fives and tens, and a few twenties, too. Before school, Mars and I stopped by Jolly Boys. I bought enough candy, snack cakes and Capri Suns to fill my backpack. I had intentionally left all the contents of my backpack for school at home stuffed into the back of my closet. I had it all planned out. I knew I needed space for my haul.

While I was on my shopping spree, I was ecstatic. Not because I was about to make an impact in my classroom, but because I had almost felt like I was paying back Al, the man who owned the store, for all the previous days' merchandise I had stolen. I was young and my thinking was greatly skewed.

If you knew the level of joy I possessed, you would know that my classmates were going to love me. They would want to be friends with me once they beheld the smorgasbord I carried in my backpack.

I arrived in Ms. Guy's sixth grade class with a sinister grin on my face. I was holding the pulse of the classroom in my backpack, and I knew it. A couple of my peers could tell I was up to something because of the way I kept asking everyone what their favorite snacks and candies were. I immediately started handing out the goodies to the girls first. They were in love with me. I could not believe that my plan had actually worked.

I was indeed the big man on campus. The young women in that sixth-grade class loved me, until what they had taken from me was consumed. Then, their loving attitudes quickly changed. But I still cherished the fleeting moment of being valued by the ladies for the short period of time that it lasted.

Even after my money heist from Mr. Bell, and my classroom grocery giveaway, I was blissfully indifferent to whatever penalty awaited me. I was so focused on being liked that getting into trouble didn't even register in my mind. Besides, Mr. Bell didn't scare me. He deserved the consequences of losing the money, not me. Right?

Well, during my snack giveaway, my mother showed up to the school, inquiring about the missing money. I fervently denied any involvement or knowledge that there were even funds to be missing. But, before I knew it, my mother was digging in my pockets. She found the rest of the money that I hadn't spent at the store earlier.

"Oh my God!" she exclaimed. "You are in so much trouble, boy. Just wait until you get home. Mr. Bell is going to go ballistic."

I couldn't have cared less. I was on a mission to rebel at all costs. I had to keep my "big man on campus" persona. At that point, all my classmates were looking out the window at my mother, confronting me in the hallway. So, I couldn't start crying. I thought about the girls' eyes and the way they smiled when they ate those snack cakes I'd delivered.

My mother chose not to remove me from school that day. She settled for threats about the impending possibilities of consequences that may arise from Mr. Bell's anger and embarrassment that he had to face showing up to the school empty-handed that morning. I decided that I was not going to be subject to anymore corporal punishment. So, I came up with a plan of my own that afternoon. I honestly had a million thoughts and scenarios running through my mind about how I could escape the wrath of Mr. Bell that evening. Suddenly, I got an insane idea. I settled on a sure plan that would get me removed from our home before Mr. Bell would even have the chance to get home and punish me.

When our school day ended, my heart was racing in anticipation. All I could think of was the fact that my plan was now about to be put into action. Mars asked if we could go back to Jolly Boys to buy more snacks on our way home. I quickly refused his request and told him we had to go straight home, especially since my mother had confiscated all the remaining funds. Now, I had to take care of something urgently. My small-framed baby brother hurried alongside me as we headed to our house so I could implement my rebellious plan of action. I knew I had to do something extreme. Although I knew what I was about to do could change my life forever, I didn't like my home life. Therefore, I was willing to take my chance and roll the dice on a decision that would soon come back and slap me in the face on that dreary afternoon.

As Mars and I reached our street, I walked at a fast pace with utter anticipation of the moments that were too soon to come. I saw my neighbor, Juan, across the street playing baseball in his yard with his younger sister, Madeline. Although Juan was nine years old, we played together often. I even considered him a friend.

I raced into our house and headed directly to our kitchen. Mars was intently watching my every move. He saw me ravaging through the drawers for the perfect weapon. He asked, "DJ, what are you doing?" He was young, but he knew I was about to make a bad decision. I pulled a large chef's knife out of the drawer.

I yelled, "Somebody's about to get it and right now!" At this point, I had such a one-track mind about what I was going to do that nobody could have prevented what happened next. I was looking for trouble and I created it!

As I ran out the front door, Mars screamed and begged me to drop the knife. But my vision was set on getting across the street and in a hurry. I had already decided that I wasn't getting a whooping that day, especially over the snacks that I had given away and the money that I had stolen.

I did not storm across the street like a maniac. I simply walked into the yard and asked Juan if I was welcome to come in his yard and join their baseball game. He agreed to me joining the afternoon fun. I told Juan I would be the catcher as he was batting, and his sister was pitching the ball. As I stood behind him, I could see Mars standing behind the fence in our yard, looking bewildered. He knew about the knife I had hidden underneath my shirt. Mars never crossed the street. He just sat, watched, and waited to see what destructive manner of nature was going to unfold on our street that afternoon by the hands of his big brother.

Juan took a swing at the ball and missed the first pitch from Madeline. I did my job like a back catcher would by retrieving the missed pitch and throwing it back to Madeline for the reset. However, as Madeline began to reset for her pitch, I stood directly behind Juan, knowing the time had now come for me to make my move. After the next swing of Juan's bat, I retrieved the chef's knife from under my shirt and slashed Juan across his back. He fell to the ground and screamed out in great shocking pain. He had a blank look on his face. In between the deep gasps for air, he stared into my eyes trying to understand how this was happening by his *supposed* friend.

He screamed so loudly that his mother stormed from their house in her pink bathrobe, yelling at the top of her lungs. Her yells turned to horrid cries for her son. She threw rocks at me and cursed at me to get out of her yard immediately. Then she ran inside their house and called 911.

In the span of fifteen minutes, my life changed drastically. I had received my wish. I definitely was not going to get a whooping from Mr. Bell. The police arrived and had me in handcuffs within seconds and sat me on the ground in our front yard. That's when the reality of what I had done settled into my heart. Tears streamed down my face. I was scared. I looked at my mother and begged her to make them take the cuffs off me as she pulled up to the house from work. I could see the tires of the ambulance underneath the police car. I wondered what type of damage I had done to my friend. But none of that mattered any longer. I had committed the crime.

By that afternoon, before Mr. Bell ever made it home to confront me, I was crying my eyes out inside a juvenile detention facility in San Bernardino, California. I was facing a felony charge that could keep me locked up until the age of twenty-five: *assault with a deadly weapon with intent to do great bodily harm.* All of this had happened because I didn't want to get a whooping at home. I'd made bad decisions to steal, rebel and consume all that wasn't mine, especially food. I chose to inflict my problems and pain into the life of an innocent bystander. Now, I had to pay with my freedom.

KING'S SPOTLIGHT

I choose to be someone that matters today. I will treat people the way I want to be treated. I will show every woman in my life the love she deserves. I will not be disrespectful or hateful. I will be the example of what a young king looks like.

CHAPTER 4
THIS BOLOGNA STINKS

I wanted to be the ruler of my kingdom so badly. But I was quite premature. I bit off more than I could chew that day. On the exterior, I portrayed this tough, pre-teen rebellious hungry street thug. I most definitely was not a street thug. However, I was always hungry.

The worst part of my first night in juvenile detention was when the black, steel door that I was housed behind slid open. A woman with a deep, raspy voice gave me orders to walk to the back of my cell and face the wall with my hands up. As soon as I complied, I heard a tray being slung into my cell. I saw the shadow of this big-framed woman with curly hair in the reflection of my cell window. The door slammed shut, and her shadow disappeared.

When I turned around, I had great anticipation. I hadn't eaten since lunch earlier in the day. *Yes! Finally, food!* was my first thought. I looked down at the blue plastic tray. What my eyes beheld wasn't going to work for me. What were these people thinking? I immediately started kicking and screaming and banging on the door. I needed answers. I had clearly received someone else's tray.

The food was practically inedible. At first sight, it looked disgusting. What I was served barely passed as a sandwich in my twelve years of living. The wheat bread was so dry that it resembled two square croutons covering one slice of discolored, stinky bologna. I didn't have any condiments to moisten the sandwich. All I had was an inner turmoil caused by the thought that this was *dinner*.

I cried more tears about that disgusting sandwich on my first night locked up than I did for my felony charge, which led to me eating my new reality. I took the first bite of the sandwich and I gagged. The bologna tasted sour and the bread scratched the roof of my mouth. However, I chewed with tears streaming down my face, hoping my tears would reach the crevices of the bread and moisten the regret of my decisions. I realized in that moment that I had made a grave mistake.

In my cell, a lightbulb went off. I realized that I wanted nothing more than to be home with my family, eating my mom's home cooking and recovering from the pain of the whooping I would have received from Mr. Bell for my antics. However, I had no such luck.

I was now starving as my heart raced into the night. All I could worry about was eating like this forever. My grandmother's dogs ate better than that three times a day. So, I went to sleep with my stomach in full growl on the first night in my new jail apartment. I was forced to sleep on a bed, which really was a cement platform, that held a paper-thin, plastic preschool mattress that deflated once I laid my heavy frame down onto it.

My unwise thinking on that day changed my life. How did I think I could create havoc and damage someone else's life, just to avoid the temporary in-house punishment of my own causing? Yet now, my lack of sound decision-making had sealed my fate as a ward of the State of California. My life became like Play-Doh in their hands, allowing them to do with me as they wished.

KING'S SPOTLIGHT

Don't you want to make a difference? Be the change we need in this world. It lives in you, young king. You are a future world leader and as you continue reading this book, I encourage you to make a declaration to take your stand now. We are depending on your next decision, to be the best decision for your life.

CHAPTER 5
CRIMINAL COURT

I remained in my cell for the first seventy-two hours in utter dread before my first court appearance. I was shackled and handcuffed with chains wrapped around my waist. I was led by detention officers, taking one-inch steps to a holding tank that held twenty-five juvenile offenders—all awaiting their initial hearings.

Although, I was young, I looked older than twelve because of my excess weight. Once in the holding tank, I discovered that many of the other offenders were up for murder and rape charges. I was terrified as I quickly realized this was the criminal big leagues.

Despite my fear, I purposely acted rebellious as I was being led into court to face the judge. I thought it made me look tough and cool. If the other offenders heard about how tough I was, and they feared me, maybe they wouldn't mess with me. But that wasn't the case.

"Mr. Powell?" the judge called. I just stared at her with an evil smirk on my face. "Are you aware of the seriousness of your charges?"

I responded, "I don't care."

My mother stood and gasped for air. Tears fell down her face when the bailiff reminded her that she couldn't have an outburst in court. She cried and shouted, "D.J.!" She received a final warning that she couldn't make any verbal outbursts in the court or else she would be removed. The judge told her to remain seated at all times.

Because of my disposition, the judge remanded me immediately back to the detention facility. The judge said I was a danger to society and myself. Staying locked up was the effective change I needed, according to the judge. This was the time to choose life over death, faith over fear. But, most importantly, I realized that it only took one second and one decision to ruin the rest of my life. Now, I was faced with just that possibility.

Tears rolled down my cheeks because I saw that I had broken my mother's heart. Whenever I saw her cry, I would cry. But honestly, I didn't care because I still felt betrayed by her for deciding to marry Mr. Bell.

As the detention officers walked me away from the courtroom, they tried to inflict mass fear into my mind. They informed me that I was going to be leaving the holding tanks and would be transferred to an actual unit, where all the bad stuff normally happens throughout the institution. There, it was an entire community of different gangs, belief systems, and morals—all dwelling in tight spaces together.

Open your eyes, young king. The world is looking for ways to destroy your mind each day. Please know that your hopes and dreams are real. Your mental awareness of who you are, and the value you hold to this world, needs to be implemented right now. The world needs your voice and your mind!

Take your stand!

KING'S
SPOTLIGHT

9 keys to Young King living

1. Remember you have a legacy on the line
2. Always remain respectful towards humanity
3. Focus your energy on what matters
4. Don't react to people who are trying to devalue you
5. Build your character daily
6. Show love with words and actions
7. Be the change in the room
8. Learn something new every day
9. Walk with your head held high

CHAPTER 6
UNIT 13
(MAXIMUM
SECURITY)

After it was decided that I was a danger to others, my life as a juvenile inmate really began. Until then, I had been housed in the holding tank of the main building.

They will decide what happens with your life because of one split-second decision. One stupid decision has cost many their freedom and lives. It's the worst position to be in. All I could think at this point was, *Maybe I should have just taken the whopping.* But it was too late. I was on my way to my new home.

There were thirteen units on the campus of the San Bernardino County Juvenile Detention Center. Unit 13 was the worst. It was the maximum-security unit. While in the holding tank, I'd heard whispers about the different units through conversations with past offenders. As they talked amongst themselves, they wished for better placement. But Unit 13 always came up. It was known as the high-crime violation unit. It housed some of California's youngest hardened criminals and gang members. I knew that couldn't be where they were sending me. To my surprise, I was very wrong.

I remember being led across the campus, passing all the less-violent units I could have only hoped for. I was moving at the same one inch per step, feeling so scared as I was being dragged by the heaviness of my weighted shackles. My heart raced a million miles a minute. I was terrified, but I couldn't show fear. I was a lost, hurting, and scared twelve-year-old little boy who had committed a violent crime. Now, I was going to be housed with the scariest juveniles our region had to offer.

It was mid-morning when we walked onto the unit. Everything was in full swing for the day. There were wards outside doing daily physical education, while others were inside attending school. During my time in the holding tank, I hadn't seen people freely walking around. They weren't playing games, having face-to-face conversations, or using the phone. But unit life was different. Whenever they weren't on lockdown because of a fight or major infraction caused by the intense gang activity on the unit, they had more freedom.

As soon as I marched onto Unit 13, with my shackles dragging and making a disturbing clinking sound, fellow inmates gave me the death stare. There was so much gang affiliation going on that they didn't know if the new guy was someone who they may have had a street beef with or just a common enemy. Neither was the case for me, but that didn't matter. Within one hour of arriving on the unit, I suffered humiliation and bullying.

Since I didn't want to follow the rules of my home, I was now subject to restrictions on when I could use the bathroom, shower, eat, talk, move, and sleep. Was my crime worth it? Absolutely not! It was the stupidest decision I could have ever made. All I kept hearing in my mind was the judge telling me that she was ready to keep me locked up until I was twenty-five years old because of my brash attitude during the court proceedings.

KING'S
SPOTLIGHT

We are in some of the most dire times in our nation's history and you, young king, have your back pressed against the wall. I know it's hard to understand and make sense of everything that is happening right before your eyes but it's not the end. Your time to rise from the ashes of generations of defeat is now. Take your stand!

CHAPTER 7
13TH BIRTHDAY

You know the feeling you get when you wake up the morning of your birthday? There is much anticipation and excitement about what the day will bring because it's *your day*. Can't nobody tell you nothing!

Well, I didn't feel much of that when I opened my eyes the morning of my thirteenth birthday. I awakened on a flat mattress that was killing my young back. I whimpered like a caged songbird without a song. The worst part for me was that I knew eating birthday cake wasn't on my agenda for the day. That thought sucked the life out of me.

My birthday breakfast consisted of powdered eggs, two pieces of burned toast with no butter, and three small, discolored sausage patties, which tasted and felt like chewing on a rubber band. I was devastated. That wasn't a birthday breakfast fit for a young king. However, I wasn't operating as a young king at the time. I was currently being served what I deserved. After all, Juan didn't deserve to be the victim of my actions.

The afternoon of my birthday, I took a trip to the common room. It was quite noisy, with the TV blaring, guys laughing and many inmates cursing the day away. I saw others gathered and battle rapping, while some focused on their daily workouts. I decided to play ping pong.

However, the birthday fun that I greatly needed came to a screeching halt. I was in the middle of a ping pong match with Trak. Trak was sixteen years old and had been sentenced to three life terms for participating in the brutal murder of an entire family. He was simply awaiting to be transferred to The California Youth Authority (CYA) in Chino, California. CYA is a high-max center for California's most serious youth and young adult offenders.

Trak was up four points in the middle of our match when, in my peripheral vision, I noticed someone running toward me. I was hit so hard on the side of my head that I passed out. I woke up in the hospital off the grounds of the detention center. I had a concussion and a headache that lasted for three days. I was told that the reason he knocked me out was because I had stolen some peanut butter crackers out of his cell. That was true, but I couldn't figure out who had snitched on me. That was the worst possible entryway into my teenage years.

Life on lockdown was not going to be better than life at home, as I had originally anticipated. In fact, when I woke up in the hospital, I realized this newfound life on Unit 13 was actually going to be a living hell on earth. I regretted the way I had treated Mr. Bell and the way I was disrespecting my mother. My actions had now left Mars at home, without me as his big brother to cover him.

I wanted to get out so bad that I cried every night, wallowing in regret as I stared at the dirt stained ceiling. I made up songs to the orchestra of sounds that took place in my stomach, resonating off the reverb of my hunger pangs. However, my decisions had already locked me in. Now, the state was able to decide what, when or how my life was going to play out from that point on. All I could do was sit and cry, while waiting month after month for something, or someone, to rescue me.

KING'S
SPOTLIGHT

Block out the noise. I know it's getting louder and harder to hear yourself think. This is just a test of your character. You can do it. You can be it. Start dreaming it.

CHAPTER 8
ARIZONA BOYS' RANCH

Thirteen years old. Less than a year before my incarceration, I was buying friends with stolen snacks, simply to avoid the name calling and bullying that I faced every day at school.

Now, I was forced to attend the juvenile detention school with gang members and murderers. I wished I could have just been back in elementary school instead of being locked down. Now, I had to be tested and cycled through the justice system. But I had to make the choice to be a rebel without a cause.

I had a Class 1 Felony in the State of California, and the judge was very stern. She assured me that if I did not complete a placement program without fail, I would be remanded immediately to CYA, where I would serve my full sentence to the age of twenty-five years of old, without early release.

I was excited at the thought of being able to leave the facility and get a chance at redemption. I was interviewed by several facilities throughout California. But the interview that scared me the most was the Arizona Boy's Ranch. This facility was infamous for coming to California and scooping up young delinquents, and taking them down to the ranch with the forward knowledge that they would not be cut out for the program. I saw many boys leave Unit 13 on their way to the ranch, only to fail within days. The treatment was so shocking to one's system.

This place was *no joke*. Imagine coming off the streets with your bad attitude in tow. You don't like being told what to do or how to do it. Your first reaction is to clap back rather than to shut your mouth. Next thing you know, you're on your way to the middle-of-nowhere Arizona. As soon as you get off the bus, your head is shaved, and drill sergeants are so close to your face that you know what they ate for breakfast. Shock quickly sets in when most wards arrive and realize that they are practically in The United States Marine Corps. The program itself is designed to break you and then rebuild you. But with the drill sergeants requiring long-distance runs, and rigorous exercises and expectations on the first day, many just choose to take their prison sentences—just like I'd chosen to commit a crime to get locked up. I thought the grass would be greener on the other side of the bars. Many faulty decisions are made when you lay down your crown.

While on Unit 13, I saw eight people return from Arizona, looking like fresh military recruits. Their long faces told the entire story of their short-lived journey of traveling to Arizona for a haircut. Many had to face the dreaded result of being transferred to CYA because they had failed to successfully complete the placement program that was offered them. I was determined not to allow that to become my fate.

KING'S SPOTLIGHT

Today I have the chance to become greater than yesterday's defeats. If I apply the knowledge and wisdom that I've learned along the way, I can accomplish every and anything I wish. Tomorrow is not promised, but I can make an impact today that can change the world forever.

I am a young king and I matter, even when I don't feel it. I am strong and have a legacy that will last if I do what's right. I will access all that is awaiting me in this life because my voice matters to the world.

CHAPTER 9
RANCH INTERVIEW

Recruiters from the Arizona Boys' Ranch came to the San Bernardino County Juvenile Detention Center once a month to interview and transport potential new wards.

Everyone who was housed on Unit 13 who had been awaiting placement were aware when the ranch staff was on the premises. Everyone had an extra level of anxiety, hoping they wouldn't hear their name called for an interview. Then...

"Mr. Powell, you're being interviewed today!"

Oh, no! I thought. *This is absolutely horrible!* I couldn't believe it. I nervously walked into the

41

meeting. But I had to think quick. *What can I do for them to not like me?*

I tried to act as hard as I possibly could. My heart raced a million miles a minute. At the point of my interview, I had been locked up on Unit 13 for months. I'd become a sponge to the war stories of what true gangster street life was like, although I had no experience in reality of the streets.

I marched into that interview like I wasn't fazed. However, I could barely run a full lap during our workouts on the basketball court. So, I knew full well that I wouldn't be able to complete five-mile runs every morning. I was afraid that going to the ranch would be a sure guarantee for my inevitable transfer to a lonely cell awaiting me at CYA for the next twelve years.

Two very large drill sergeants with buzzed haircuts awaited me in the room for our interview. I walked in with a smirk on my face. That was normally the way I dealt with my emotions. I often deflected through humor. But that clearly wasn't the environment for cheers.

The first drill sergeant locked eyes with me and immediately started yelling, "Your life is on the line, boy! This ain't no smiling matter!" That certainly removed the smirk from my face instantly. "Did you hear me?" he asked again in an angered tone.

I responded, "Yeah, man. I hear you."

Immediately, they both jumped up and stood on either side of my face panting like angry dogs. They both screamed and spit in my face as they said, "You call us sir! Do you understand, boy?"

I said, "I'm no boy. Stop spitting on me." I was giving them the worst possible attitude I could muster. Once I witnessed the aggression in this small room, there was no way in hell that I wanted to leave that facility with those scary beasts.

Their faces were as red as apples. One of them screamed at the top of his lungs, "You damn sure ain't no man! You ain't nothing but a fat punk who ain't gonna do shit with his life!" I couldn't hold back the tears welling up in my eyes. I had heard those same words before in the past. They resonated deep within the abyss of my soul. My plan had backfired once again. Now, I was feeling so low, like the failure I already knew I had become. I'd only lived on the earth for thirteen years. At that point, it seemed as if CYA may have been Disney Land compared to being placed at the ranch.

They tag teamed me and wouldn't stop berating me. "I heard you slashed someone, you dumb faggot. Slash me, you black sucker!" The taunting continued for almost fifteen minutes until I fell to the floor crying. I couldn't take the pressure any longer.

One of the sergeants yelled, "Just what I thought! You're just another black statistic and we don't want you on our ranch." Then they kicked me out of the room. I was so relieved that they didn't want me. It felt like I had a brand-new lease on life, but I was still faced with the thought and the reality that I was a failure, and nobody wanted me. So, I went from being happy that they didn't want me to being sad that I was still in the same situation. I didn't know if *anyone* would ever want me.

KING'S
SPOTLIGHT

If I give love, love will always find its way back to me. My value is set by my character and how I make decisions each day. So today, I will choose wisely and exhibit kingly character.

CHAPTER 10
VISITING SNACKS

I lived in daily hunger and misery on Unit 13 for two more months before I was interviewed again for placement. I wanted a chance at redemption. I prayed every day that someone would come to rescue me out of the pit I was now faced with living, even though I was there because of my own choosing and doing. I knew for sure that I didn't want to go to CYA, but my options and time were both running out.

We were only allowed visitors a couple times a week. My mother would come for the visits. She was my sole visitor for the entire time I was locked up. The times she visited were the greatest moments I had while being in Unit 13. She sat at the assigned table for our visit with a brown bag full of snacks from the canteen. She also brought me comic books and coloring books to help me pass the time.

My mom was always inquisitive about the other inmates' backstories and what crimes they had committed to be placed on Unit 13. I filled her in about things I had learned and acts that my fellow wards had committed. Most times she listened with her mouth agape. She wondered how her thirteen-year-old son was now living in such a place with the likes of murderers and rapists.

I loved my mother's visits. I also loved sharing stories with her. But I loved the snacks more because the food I was forced to eat every day was so disgusting. I savored each crumb I was able to consume that wasn't produced on the grounds of 900 E. Gilbert St.

I was required to eat all snacks she brought in by the time our visits were over. One of the older wards on the unit taught me how to hoard snacks for later consumption in my room. He only charged me a pack of Starbursts for the lesson. He showed me how to cut a slit into the lining of my sweatshirt using the corner grate on the window in my cell.

I would funnel the snacks into the lining of my sweatshirt. That is until one day when I got caught and lost all visiting privileges for the remainder of my sentence.

I will never forget the failure bomb that was dropped in my nude lap as I stood there in a bathroom full of naked teens shaking their clothes out. I took a gentle shake of my sweatshirt, but I forgot when I was giving my hoarding lesson that I was supposed to secure the snacks with my hand wrapped around the band of my sweatshirt. All the learned criminal knowledge quickly departed my head. I was so focused on how I was going to make love to those snacks once I got them into my cell. However, I had no such luck that day when two Snickers, a Butterfinger, and a pack of Starburst went tumbling to the ground right at the guard's feet.

Despair set in. I had really blown it. I felt like I was all alone. I didn't have anyone to visit me anymore. I needed my mother more than anything. But because of that one decision months earlier of trying to avoid Mr. Bell's whooping, my dominoes were falling and life itself became a desperate plea for answers. I was a young king with no hope and no snacks.

CHAPTER 11
OAKLAND IS CALLING!

One morning, my unit counselor advised me that a group home had called to inquire if I was still locked up and seeking placement. He assured them that I was, but then he informed me that the only potential problem was that R&L Children's Home was nearly 450 miles away in Oakland, California.

He said, "Mr. Powell, someone is out there looking out for you!" Just the sound of him relaying that message gave me a glimmer of hope that I hadn't had in a long time.

After six months of being locked up on Unit 13, I was finally placed without a formal interview. I was told that I had one week to prepare to depart. I told them immediately that I didn't need a week.

I was ready that day. However, that was their process. I'm not sure if I was happier to be leaving the facility so I could eat a real meal, or to finally be able to breathe the air outside of detention. Both options sounded like a day in paradise compared to the six months I had just experienced.

When that amazing morning came, I heard, "Mr. Powell, pack up your stuff. You're getting out of here today." It was a Tuesday morning at 4:30 a.m. The night guard's frame filled my cell window. All I could see was his shadow.

I rubbed the sleep from my eyes and asked, "Am I going home?"

He replied, "I doubt you're going home, but you're getting the hell out of here."

He handed me a clear trash bag for my belongings. I didn't have much, but I frantically tossed everything from that cell into my bag.

Finally! I thought. *I'm getting placed.* I knew this was my only chance to prove to the judge that I was worth rehabilitation. Although I was excited, I was also terrified. My judge was known to be one of the staunchest at sticking to her word about sentencing.

I was led to a meeting room where I was told to sit and wait. I sat at the table and assumed the nap position for a short period of time. I was awakened by the sound of someone singing *Let's Groove To-night* by Earth, Wind & Fire. I looked up and saw this dark-skinned man with a Jheri curl walking toward me with a great bright smile on his face.

For many months, everyone I interacted with, including the guards, was either angry, mean, hateful, or despondent. So, to be in this room with a man who was singing and cheerful at 5 a.m. immediately put me at ease.

He shook my hand and introduced himself as Bryan. He never berated me or talked down to me. He simply chatted with me like a normal human being.

He asked, "You ready to leave this dump?"

I answered in the most affirmative way that I could that early, "Heck, yes!" After all the logistics and paperwork had been signed to transfer custody to Oakland, we walked out the front doors by 6 a.m. We were both singing, "Let's groove tonight!"

CHAPTER 12

THE BEST THING I'VE EVER EATEN

As we drove to Northern California, Bryan encouraged me and did all he could to try and erase the layers of labels placed on me during my incarceration. During that eight-hour drive, Bryan kept reminding me that I still had a choice for my life. I didn't have to believe the lies of naysayers and adversaries. He pleaded with me to not become another statistic. I also discovered that Bryan was the manager of one of the R&L locations. In fact, he was the nephew of the owner.

Before heading to Oakland, we stopped for breakfast at IHOP. Bryan told me I could order anything I wanted from the menu. My mouth watered as I opted for a double full stack of eight pancakes and a steak omelet with extra cheese. As I sat there, salivating after every bite, I had vivid flashbacks of my last six months of dining displeasures. This, by far, was the best food I'd eaten in my thirteen years.

Bryan continued to talk as we ate. "You, my friend, are indeed a young king." I just stared at him. He could tell I really wasn't following. He continued, "You don't understand. You are thirteen years old. The State of California Department of Justice is making decisions for your life."

I took another bite.

"Dexter, when are you going to take your stand?"

"What stand?" I asked.

He replied, "How are you going to get your voice back?"

It was too early in the morning for this dude's energy. I was starting to get annoyed. Every time he asked me a question, I had to look up from my plate. But there was something about him and his spirit that I liked. Frankly, I knew he was right. I could tell he wanted me to see something inside of myself that I couldn't yet see. I told him I didn't understand fully, but I appreciated him.

He responded, "We're about to get in the car and drive for eight hours. We are going to sing, laugh and have a good time. Cool?" I looked across the table and smiled. Bryan then said, "Hold your head up. Stand tall, young king, and take your stand. Let's ride out!"

KING'S SPOTLIGHT

I understand that by society's standards I am deemed a threat because of the color of my skin. I haven't even had a chance to live and people have already given up on me. I am a difference maker. I am a free thinker and I hold the key to many possibilities.

CHAPTER 13
NEW CITY, NEW CHANCE

When I arrived in Oakland with my clear trash bag, and blue-and-white detention-issued uniform on, I was ready for change. But I also didn't know what awaited me in Oakland, just like I didn't know the full scope of what awaited me on Unit 13.

We pulled up to a large facility that housed 40 boys. Although the residents were all sizes and shapes, their community closet didn't have any clothes to fit me that day. In a matter of moments, the residents began whispering about me and the fact that I couldn't fit any of the clothes. The news spread throughout the floors of the group home. This resulted in me being teased right away by many of the older kids. They were looking for fresh meat to grind.

I heard one Hispanic teen, who was standing in the hall outside the closet, say very loudly, "Look at this dumb ass fatso! He can't even fit normal clothes." It felt like the vicious cycle of bullying was following me everywhere I went. I frowned and responded by throwing a personal jab back into his direction. But it fell short and I became even more embarrassed.

The owner of the group home shut down the extra attention. She could see that I was overwhelmed by the onslaught of voices aimed in my direction. That afternoon, Mrs. Lewis took me to a men's big and tall store and bought me four pairs of pants, underwear, socks, undershirts, four button-up shirts and some nice new shoes. It felt like something I would have done with my mother had I been back at home.

I was so thankful that she cared enough to take me to a specialty shop for clothes because she knew a normal Sears wasn't going to cut it for my large frame. When we arrived back at the group home, and the other residents saw my bags in tow, I was repeatedly told that I wasn't special just because I was fat. I was reminded not to think that I was going to get attention like that every day, because I wasn't.

Each day after I arrived, I was bullied. I had to defend myself from numerous attacks, both verbal and physical. These people didn't know me, yet

I had learned great gangster language. I vowed to react immediately if the residents started with me. They did often. So, I acted crazy to throw them off. I did something I hadn't done before, which was start swinging as soon as the first words came out of their mouths. I balled my fist up and aimed right where I would hear them forming their words. After three documented in-house assault charges in Oakland, they decided to send me to another R&L home in Fremont, California. They wanted to see if it would be a better fit as opposed to sending me back to the detention facility, which would have landed me in CYA. I was so grateful that I had received yet another chance.

There was one major difference between the two homes. The home in Oakland housed around 40 boys between the ages of thirteen and eighteen. The home in Fremont, which only housed six boys, seemed like it would be a breeze.

On the day I was transferred to my new home in Fremont, I was so excited because I wasn't being transferred back to Southern California. When we pulled up to the house, I was surprised that it was an actual four-bedroom home with a pool in a residential neighborhood. Although there were only six boys in the house, the dynamics and complications mounted up quickly.

My initial meeting with the residents was pretty cool. Nobody called me any names. I didn't feel the need to ball up my fist. I thought this place would actually work for me.

Bryan, to my surprise and amazement, was the house manager for the Fremont group home. I was so excited. The person who had told me that I was a young king was going to be able to walk with me through every step of the journey I was now on.

Every night, we followed a specific program that was geared at keeping everyone accountable for their thoughts and actions. During our group discussions, we talked about any and all household problems and we updated level statuses. Then, we would be released to do our nightly chores.

It didn't take long for me to realize that, in Fremont, if you did what was required, you'd pretty much float through the program and finish successfully. Bryan didn't want any of us to fall into the school-to-prison pipeline. So, I planned to set myself apart, rise up and take my stand, regardless of how I felt day to day.

Young king, your emotions have the ability to make you react and do things that you said or thought you would never do. It doesn't have to be this way. You have control of your internal barometer, which guides you into knowing what's right and wrong. You can arise and take your stand!

CHAPTER 14
I'LL TAKE
THE KITCHEN

I became addicted to food at seven years old. That's when I first grew from a cute husky boy to overweight. I always wanted to be around the food so I could secretly indulge in it. When I arrived in Fremont, I saw an opportunity to do just that and I put that plan into action.

Up until this point, every time I had a plan of action, it backfired on me. But I was pretty confident in this plan. Although my motives were selfish, I knew I would be able to create change in the house and make others feel good if it worked out in my favor.

Each week, every resident was assigned a chore. Our chores list included cleaning the bathroom, living room, outside clean-up, and pool maintenance. There was also kitchen duty and cleaning up after meals. A few other small tasks were required daily from everyone.

My third week of being in Fremont, I was assigned kitchen duty. I read the description on the book:

Client that has kitchen duty performs the following: picks meal and follows recipe, preps all items, serving of residents, and you are responsible for washing all the dishes that you used for your meal.

The first day I was assigned to kitchen duty, I made my grandmother's meatloaf. It was the best meatloaf that I had personally ever tasted, and all the others agreed. Joe, one of the other residents, said, "You need to cook every night from now on."

Another resident, Steve, raised his hand from across the table and said, "I second that." That very day, food didn't just consume my life. It also gave me life and a renewed purpose. Before, I'd never felt valued or needed. Now, these people were enjoying my food. That established value on the inside of me.

Everyone decided to divide the remaining chores amongst themselves. They designated me as the resident cook. I was thrilled to know that I would never have to clean the nasty bathrooms. They gave me creative freedom in the kitchen, and it worked for me. I gladly stayed on my kitchen duty for another eighteen months until I reached Level 4 of the program.

Level 4 was the top level of achievement. It was a highly sought-after position on the ladder to successfully completing your state placement. With the newfound love that I received in the kitchen, and my ability to change atmospheres with creations, my behavior drastically changed. The image I had of myself also changed. I moved through my levels at a different speed than everyone else. I reached Level 4 a full six months earlier than scheduled because I wasn't getting in trouble. I was focused on providing scrumptious meals each day. Suddenly, my crown began to shine brighter.

I grew and matured while living in Fremont. I was living in my purpose. Each day, I'd walk into the kitchen with my apron on to prepare a new meal for my peers. I always had a great excitement about my creative flow for the evening.

I held my head high, like Bryan always reminded me to. I realized that, yes, I did make a terrible judgment call that I was now paying the consequences for. But it didn't have to be my final chapter in life. It didn't have to label me forever, like the two Arizona buzzed cut bullies did to me. I realized that what Bryan told me all those months earlier was true. I was indeed a young king with royal blood flowing through my veins. I was ready to rise and take my stand. The journey that I had to walk through because of my criminal charge wasn't easy. Life isn't easy, especially when you cause unnecessary drama in your own life. But I realized I had a choice moving forward. I had to choose the road that led to greater kingdom heights.

I spent a total of 19 months in R&L Children's Home. Although I had my kitchen duty, which I found self-value in, I still wanted to be seen by my peers. I wanted them to like me. So, I was often influenced to remove my crown and participate in activities that could have easily allowed me to be thrown into adult prison. I was a follower at the time, not a leader.

When you remove your crown to follow someone into a pit, you can't get scared of the dark when your light gets snuffed out!

Life gets tough. Yes, we will make many mistakes in life. We will make some bad decisions, too. But even then, we can either continue to rebel against what we know is right and leave our entire existence in the hands of a courtroom, or find ourselves staring down the barrel of someone's gun if we don't take an immediate stand.

Rise up, young king! Rise! Take your stand!

CHAPTER 15
NEXT IS NOW

I was terrified to go home because it meant I had to face Mr. Bell. He and my mom had married, and he was my stepfather. My decision kept me from celebrating many momentous occasions with family and friends, all because I didn't want to suffer the consequences for stealing the fundraiser money. Little did I understand at the time that Mr. Bell's punishment would have been swift, and it would have left me without a criminal record.

Upon my release, I was on strict probation. I still had my pre-existing felony hanging over my head daily. I could hear the judge's voice playing roundabouts in my head, "Mr. Powell, I better not see you before you turn eighteen years old, unless you are coming in here to change someone's life for the better."

The latter part of her statement resonated with me. I wondered what she meant by "...change someone's life..." A year after I was released from R&L, I received a call from the owners, asking if they could fly me back to Oakland to share my story at their annual camp retreat. They wanted all the campers to hear the testimony of my life and the restoration process. I already had a voice, even though I was scared to use it.

It seemed so crazy and juvenile. To think, I was the kid who had nearly thrown his entire life away to avoid a temporary in-home punishment for my actions.

I cried more tears than a little bit about my actions. But the thing about actions is that, once you act, it's on. There is an equal reaction to every action, whether it's good or bad. My actions at twelve years old changed the way I thought. I was forced to grow up faster than I needed to. My mind wasn't mature. I received street growth and an unwanted education of how to be a thug from the ones who thought it was vital to teach all others around them the level of their thuggery.

I tried hard to improve and prove myself daily when I was in the system. More than anything, I became trapped and I wanted out, but it was too late. I was so grateful for the opportunity to live at R&L Children's Home and to find and develop my passion for cooking food for others. Seeing them enjoy it brought me the greatest satisfaction.

When I received the invitation to speak, I was sixteen years old. I also weighed 350 pounds. Although I was thrilled at the thought of going back to speak to the residents, I had constant ravaging thoughts in my mind about how unworthy I was. As I stood in the mirror looking at my reflection, I was reminded of my reality: I was fat and ugly. *Are people going to listen to me and take me seriously?* I considered declining the invitation because of my fear. But, after talking it over with my mom during dinner, I decided I to accept.

I remember feeling like a boss getting dropped off at the airport at that young age. It really felt like a dream. Even after all my trouble, and all that had previously tried to destroy me, my crown was intact. I was ready to establish my voice and domain in the world.

That hot, sunny summer afternoon, I nervously stood before 175 boys, who were staring down my throat. I focused on the blue sky. It looked like a freshly painted canvas. The lake glistened like flakes of crystal in the sun. I wasn't perfect by any means. There should have been a million other speakers there that afternoon to motivate the boys, but they'd chosen me. I stood before them, willing my mouth to utter something, anything. Every word of motivation drained from my brain.

I was morbidly obese, and I lacked confidence at all levels. As I stood on the platform, I heard snickering and small talk coming from the crowd of campers. Past memories invaded my soul.

My life had been full of anxiety. I was a sad kid who lacked friends and character. It caused me to become troubled from the very beginning. I lost all control of myself, and I almost lost everything in the process. Sweat dripped down my brow and I was speechless. The movie of my life played from the moment I attacked Juan. Then, I saw the entire arrest sequence and the food I was served, especially that stinky bologna sandwich. I thought of all the gallons of tears I'd cried because of the internal pain of repeating the same cycles yet expecting different results.

The different results never found me. I had a voice at sixteen and I had a chance to use it. I had been standing on this platform for nearly five minutes and it was getting harder for me to speak. As I surveyed the crowd I realized that they were waiting to hear what I was going to say. Suddenly, it came to me.

I pictured myself walking out of the juvenile detention facility that first morning and going to IHOP with Bryan. I remembered his face as he stared into my eyes so passionately with love and support. I recalled his testimony of recovery from addiction to crack cocaine. Then, I channeled his morning energy and with my loudest voice possible, I screamed across the entire lake so everyone could hear: "Young kings, arise and take your stand!"

CHAPTER 16 ·
OUR NEW REALITY

Unfortunately, in this mass racially insensitive society we live in, as black men, the moment our soul leaves our front doorstep, we become victimized by the stigma in society. That stigma is about who we are as a people and our distinct pigmentations that we each rightfully possess.

We have become a dying breed because of the way we look, think, act, and breathe. This is going to be a battle that we will face every day for the rest of our lives.

Driving a vehicle should be something simple we do that carries us from point A to point B, without concern for making it to our destination. But, in our new reality, driving has become one of the most dangerous and stressful things a black man can do in America.

Most will never understand the magnitude of driving while black, with divided focus on the road ahead and the cops behind. Our psychological systems cause shock that suddenly renders us unable to focus solely on the road ahead. We become so consumed with looking back and not being stopped. Even when driving clean, our minds quickly inventory the contents of the vehicle.

We become ravaged by these uncontrollable thoughts and our pulse quickens. Consumed with being the perfect driver, we may make a sudden turn and forget to put on the turn signal. The inevitable happens. The flashing lights in the rear-view mirror conjure images of the hundreds of news stories.

We find ourselves having this brush with the law for driving while under the intoxication of them on our minds. These scenarios always play into their favor before they will ever fall into ours.

So, always be aware of your surroundings. Utilize your camera phone to record all interactions with police that concern you. Know that you are highly necessary in our current climate. So, rise and shine like the young king you are.

Our people have been under attack for hundreds of years. You, young king, have come into another generation of the battle for your life, liberty, and the pursuit of happiness. Many people of color are under attack across America. But the pursuit of the black man has now turned into a witch-hunt for our souls.

Yes, we are in the most complex and complicated times of our nation's history. Many who have taken vows to protect and serve us have also taken unspoken secret vows to kill us under the protection of their badges as shields.

We are judged the moment they know we possess an ounce of black blood in our bodies. Our stock, according to the world's system, diminishes like a new car driven off the lot. It's no longer worth its original value. That is what has happened because of our skin color. We are instantly devalued before anyone learns our true value. Their life's journey could be changed for the better if they would simply give someone the decency of seeing them for who they are and who they were created to be. Their lives could be changed for the better if they were not so focused on looking for mistakes, flaws, or pigment. But our world's systems are crooked, and they are not set in our favor.

Young king, you must remain the example of character, not the projected disposition of shame the world wants you to carry for being born in the skin you're in!

KING'S SPOTLIGHT

As a king I will stand with the young kings as I pledge to not allow my past hurts to dictate how I mentor and show love to the boys who look like me, sound like me, and possess the same hurts as me. I won't let up, give up, or give in to the pressures of this world to abandon my position as a king mentor. I have been hurt, so I know how hurt feels and I will do my best not to impart those same feelings that I felt as a young king into the young kings that I have taken under my wings.

CHAPTER 17
CALL TO ACTION

Where are the young kings who are willing to stand up and say, "Enough is enough" and mean it? We wear our loved one's faces on our white tees and shed mad tears at their funerals. But, then what? When will the violence stop? When will we stop killing one another? When will *they* stop killing us? Countless young black lives are lost daily in cities across America and little is being done to stop it.

I want to encourage you to stand for what's right. All money ain't good money. Show love with your words and love will find its way to you.

Do not give up or make *forever* decisions based on *temporary* circumstances. Trouble doesn't last always. This too shall pass. You are a young king, my friend, of a royal bloodline. Arise in this world and take your place.

Treat our queens with the utmost respect. They definitely deserve it. They are the reason we have entry into this earth. Even under stress, you don't have the right to demean a young lady and call her out of her name. Yes, I am aware that many of the songs you listen to, and many young ladies even, demean themselves. But you shouldn't join the party. Don't diminish your value in the process.

It's time to focus on yourself and get to a place in life where you determine that, no matter the circumstances, you are going to try your absolute best to be the most authentic young king the world needs.

It's obvious that there are many people who look at our blackness as scary and threatening, rather than beautiful and empowering. Young king, that is who we are! Our families have endured pain generation after generation. Now, we have put muzzles over our minds and eyes, and our lives have become a blur. Life is here and, before you know it, it will be over. How you live your life from this point on is what matters the most for your future!

When you die, what will they say about you? Will your legacy reflect your royal kingship? Did you help build the world up, or did you help tear it down? Did you stand against injustice, or did you merge with the masses? Who are you to the world?

To my older kings: How many of us will stand arm in arm with young black men across America? How many of us will embrace them and look them in their eyes to tell them they are indeed loved and very much needed?

We must give our young kings complete logical instruction about dealing with the daily encounters they face. Communication with adults and people of authority, such as police officers, has fallen by the wayside because nobody wants to be told what to do. The perception of one who wants to fight back will always paint the picture of being disrespectful, instead of people calling you a shining example of a young king, worthy of leading others.

Think about every time someone let you down as you were growing up. Remember the suffocating feeling that permeated your entire existence, leaving you in a pile of your own broken heart. Don't do that to our young kings who have been brought into your life for safekeeping. Our young kings are in a fight for their lives each minute of every day. One decision they may make has the potential to derail their entire purpose.

If you start the process of standing with our young kings, don't abandon them. Don't destroy their kingship by mishandling your responsibilities to stand. Consistency is key when trying to break through to the heart of our young kings. You must listen to their voices and get an understanding of how they operate on all levels. Get clarity on what causes their thought processes and what drives their emotions. Figure out what type of responses are caused because of their world insight and knowledge they currently possess.

Yes, this is going to require a life's work. But if someone would have put the same work and time into learning and understanding you while you were a young king, life would have been different. Many of the burdens you still deal with could have been dealt with years ago if you'd only had a little extra love and attention in your life.

Let's do something different. Make a vow that we will not repeat and pass the same cycles of brokenness to our next generations of young kings. It was done to far too many of us while we were growing up. We were often left hanging in the balance with our tears running down the skin on our faces. We searched for answers of why we were always being lied to. We wondered if anyone unconditionally loved us.

If you can take the lessons you learned during your young kingship, and sow that knowledge back into the hearts of the lost and broken young kings, you will have a rebirth in your own heart. You have the opportunity to give what you never received. You have the chance to be to someone else the very person you've always needed for your own life.

This is how we evoke great change in the hearts of our young kings. Always be present, no matter what the day may bring or what they may say to you that may trigger something within you.

There is great hurt that lives in so many of our young kings' hearts. They don't know how to bring expression to their pain. Thinking you can simply show up and get right into the center of their existence based on your experience isn't going to happen. The hurt and apprehension to trust doesn't get locked into one's soul in one season. So, the magnitude of silent hurt living within someone can cause most to build walls, which seem impossible to scale in the beginning. However, this is not the time to give up on our young kings. The same young king who you take a stand for today will one day have a rightful place designed just for you in their library of hope and restoration—all because you came, stayed, loved and didn't abandon the assignment. Never leave their side. Even old kings desire the love and encouragement they never received.

Kings from the north, south, east, and west can all stand on one accord, and hold our young kings up because this is our call. Let's arise and help them polish their crowns. Let's establish in them who they are for our world. We are implementing true grassroots change. We are more than capable to shift the power and insight of the minds of the ones who have felt totally abandoned, alone, misunderstood, and unloved.

Kings, arise! Take your stand!

CHAPTER 18
YOUR MIND MATTERS

Young king, I want these words to become the most important words you will read. Let these strong words leave a lasting impact on your life that will forever change your perspective: It's ok not to be ok.

Mental illness is real. You may be suffering in silence. Your mind may have been conditioned to hold onto your emotions until the point of explosion and you don't know what to do. Well, the process before getting to the point of explosion looks very different in everyone. Anxiety, fear, depression, cutting, over-eating, isolating, suicidal thoughts, substance abuse, all these life effects often lead to behaviors that could cause your incarceration or an early death.

I know we possess these strong manly personas for the world to see. What they can't see is what's living on the inside. They don't understand what's happening in the six inches between your ears. That silent pain you've been carrying is currently leading you to a level of exhaustion and frustration and living each day has become a chore rather than a life-sustaining purpose worthy of peace or joy.

The weight of carrying this pain has been consuming all parts of your life and the suffocation you're now experiencing will offer you no escape, if not dealt with. I am an advocate for getting professional help.

I know becoming a spectator of your own existence has left you gasping for air. You know you need help before you drown in the toxic pond your mind is floating in. But the thought of someone knowing you've been hearing or seeing things that aren't really there, would look crazy. You have this diminished public image to uphold, so you choose to remain silent, pushing you closer to becoming unraveled.

Young king now is not the time to hold onto such deep mental secrets. Your life is on the line and if you need help, it's perfectly ok. It takes a king to understand that in order for his kingdom to run smoothly, he has to accept help in the areas that he is ill-equipped. It's ok to welcome the help because, at the end of day, when the all the proper pieces are on the board and ready to operate, the true game of chess begins.

Amid your sleepless nights and inability to focus, you've failed to see that there is help available. But you must first voice your pain through the proper channels. There are those who are waiting to service you towards a better future. You need to find someone you can trust (i.e., coach, mentor, parent, spiritual leader, teacher, school counselor) who can direct you to the proper resources, while walking with you, on the journey towards healing your mind, body, and soul.

I know that mental health is a taboo topic in our African American culture, but we must take back control of our lives. It starts with admitting that you're not alright and then be willing to get your mental health game back together, one decision at a time. You know when the coach tells you "keep your head in the game" that mantra rings so true to all aspects of your life.

We need your head in the game but how do you jump into a game of life with a broken heart and broken mind? I know you have experienced levels of hurt and pain in your young life that would make the strongest person on earth shiver. But in your pain has been living an even greater purpose for the legacy you will leave on this earth because of the moves you will make from this point forward.

Young king, these words I write will be the final pages of this book, but the words that remain living and breathing inside of your heart mean that the final chapter of your life has yet to be written. Even in the trauma that you may be facing today, if you hold on and don't give up prematurely, today's pain will one day lead you into tomorrow's purpose that you will carry to the world.

You may feel like the strands of your rope are unraveling faster than you can keep up with. The voices of others have caused you to not understand or listen to your own voice any longer. You feel like nobody understands or really even cares about what you're going through. You feel like death would end all your constant thoughts. You feel defeated before getting out of bed. You don't want to live because all you feel is death.

I have lived all these terrible emotions. I have listened to the outside voices and have allowed their words to sink into my life, which caused me severe consequences. I didn't realize that I needed help, but I did. I couldn't breathe because of my internal pain and my mind was a floating black cloud of disgruntled anger. My inability to think within reason caused my conditions to spiral out of control because the levels of my illness were getting deeper the longer I held it in. I needed professional help, but I waited because of my denial. With painful silence, I lived each day while the effects of my silence ate my mind from the inside out, I couldn't take life anymore and I reached that point of explosion that I referenced above.

I don't want that for your life young king! Suicide is not the answer. The pain is temporary even though every minute feels like a lifetime. If you are under the water in your own tears, tell someone and don't do life alone.

Take the information provided on the next page and reach out to an organization who is waiting to direct you to the available resources to help save your life and kingdom!

Young king, take your stand, today!

RESOURCE PAGE

Young King do you need Immediate Help In A Crisis?

National Suicide Prevention Lifeline – Call 800-273-TALK (8255)

If you or someone you know is in crisis—whether they are considering suicide or not—please call the toll-free Lifeline at 800-273-TALK (8255) to speak with a trained crisis counselor 24/7.

The National Suicide Prevention Lifeline connects you with a crisis center in the Lifeline network closest to your location. Your call will be answered by a trained crisis worker who will listen empathetically and without judgment. The crisis worker will work to ensure that you feel safe and help identify options and information about mental health services in your area. Your call is confidential and free.

Crisis Text Line – Text NAMI to 741-741

Connect with a trained crisis counselor to receive free, 24/7 crisis support via text message.

National Domestic Violence Hotline – Call 800-799-SAFE (7233)

Trained expert advocates are available 24/7 to provide confidential support to anyone experiencing domestic violence or seeking resources and information. Help is available in Spanish and other languages.

National Sexual Assault Hotline – Call 800-656-HOPE (4673)

Connect with a trained staff member from a sexual assault service provider in your area that offers access to a range of free services. Crisis chat support is available at Online Hotline. Free help, 24/7.

A NOTE FROM THE AUTHOR

We all face daily struggles. Because of my struggles, you are reading this book. Getting locked up at that young age made life extremely hard. The road to getting this book out has been nothing short of a miracle.

I am thirty-eight years old now. But what you don't know is that, after being released from R&L Children's Home, I went back home to my family and was integrated back into school. Although I often made bad decisions and got in a lot of trouble, I comforted myself with food and got lost in that. By the time I was eighteen, I weighed 430 pounds.

At age eighteen, I made another life-altering decision to move out of my parents' home. I decided that I was grown, and I didn't need to be disciplined any longer. Little did I know that the people I moved in with were crackheads. Less than forty-eight hours after leaving home, I became addicted to crack cocaine.

It all started from my first major decision to rebel against everything and everyone I knew was right. It cost me so much by way of relationships, money, time, and years of endless pain.

I spent my twenties, and many years into my thirties, battling the effects of that initial decision. I have suffered greatly, and I do not want this for your life, young king.

Not too long ago, I reached a point where everything I saw looked bleak, including my finances, my health, and my employment. Dwelling on negative thoughts, I tried to come up with ways to get over or come up with some resources on my own. But every time I played the entire scene in my head, it directed me right back to that sandwich with the dry wheat bread and discolored bologna.

As I wrote this book, I saw your face and felt your tears. I spent many nights unable to sleep, seeing the faces of angry black boys who have become angry men with pain that has been bottled up for years. It's okay to cry. The pain is real, and the loss is real. Your feelings are valid.

Then, I saw the faces of the ones who, unfortunately, made bad decisions and are now paying the ultimate price. They are currently incarcerated. Arise, king!

Many children have lost parents because of bad decisions like mine. I missed out on much of my daughter's life because I was chasing the wrong things. I traveled a long road, which I urge you not to follow. It's not worth it. The good news is that we can always choose to make our next decision our best decision.

I had to retrace my footsteps back to that decision at twelve years old. I thought about that breakfast with Bryan, and I knew I only had one more chance to arise and become the king who I was meant to be. I had to take my stand. So, I'm walking on water right now and you can, too.

I can't wait to see how many young kings will rise up during this movement. I can't wait to see how many of you will become voices of change and hope in our broken world.

ABOUT THE AUTHOR

Dexter A. Powell, Jr. currently resides in Michigan with his wife, Breona, and their two dogs, Ryder and Max.

His passions include culinary arts, improv acting, music artistry, and media arts.

He lives to create innovative dishes that are pleasing to the eyes and palate. His caring heart has afforded him the opportunity to become a direct care worker for seniors and those with developmental disabilities focusing on music therapy as a means towards healing.

His mission is to help young kings live out their potential despite living in a society that looks at them as second-rate citizens.

Depression and defeat were badges that Dexter carried for many years. He has now emerged as a leader who is set to change the country and the world. His transparency and direct approach to life shine through the heart and lens of love.

For booking inquiries, please visit:

www.youngkingbook.com or
email: orderyoungking@gmail.com

CPSIA information can be obtained
at www.ICGtesting.com
Printed in the USA
JSHW020335270621
16183JS00006B/10

9 781952 926037